This book is presented to:

ISBN: 978-1-4627-4273-8
Published by B&H Publishing Group, Brentwood, Tennessee

DEWEY: C220.95
SUBHD: BEDTIME \ BIBLE STORIES
Printed in Heshan, Guangdong, China, in April 2024
10 11 12 13 14 28 27 26 25 24

My Good Night® Bible

by Susan L. Lingo

Illustrated by Jacqueline East

BH KIDS

Contents

Introduction

In the hustle and bustle of today's world, it's hard to find even a few moments of peace. Quiet times together with your children are scarce and fleeting. But these can be the most important times that you spend together, especially in those precious early years of your children's lives.

My Good Night® Bible can help you make the most of the time that you have. Setting aside a special time to snuggle up and read Bible stories together is a wonderful way to let children know they are important and help them understand God's love. With *My Good Night® Bible*, you can develop a peaceful, calming bedtime routine that will help your child think about God while making an easy transition from busy day to silent night.

1. Read the Bible story to your child. One of the unique features of *My Good Night® Bible* is the age-appropriate storytelling. Each story uses short sentences and words that are familiar to a child's growing vocabulary. Alliteration, rhyme, and rhythm capture children's attention and invite them to repeat catchy story words and phrases.

2. Read the Scripture verse together. Each verse presents the theme for that story. These are verses that children can actually learn, understand, and put to use in their lives!

3. Talk to God together. Use the prayer provided or pray in your own words. Let your child say a prayer of his or her own too.

4. Say the Sleep Time word. Give your child a pleasant, God-centered thought to carry him or her through the night.

At bedtime, you have a unique opportunity for you and your child to learn about God together. Educational studies have confirmed that sleeping or resting after learning something new actually increases understanding, retention, and recall. Reading God's Word and thinking about His truth at bedtime gives children the entire night to sleep with God-centered thoughts.

God bless you, and sleep tight!

Susan Lingo

The Old Testament

God Made the World

Genesis 1:1–2:3

Who made the world? God made the world! God made light, and God made air. God made green plants everywhere. And it was good. What do you see in the world?

Who made the world? God made the world! God made the fish. God made the sky. God made animals and people. Oh my! And it was good. What do you see in the world?

Who made the world? God made the world! God made the world. God made it best. Then what did God make?

God made REST.
And it was very good.
Night-night!

God said, "I made the earth." (Isaiah 45:12)

Prayer Time

Let's thank God for all His love
and watchful care from up above.

Dear God,

Thank You for the wondrous world You made with so much love. Thank You for the earth below and for the stars above.

Amen.

Sleep Time

Tonight's Bible word is *world*. God's world is so great. What's your favorite part of the world? Sleep tight!

Adam Names the Animals

Genesis 2:18–23; 3:20

Who made the world? God made the world! Who made trees and flowers? God made trees and flowers! Who made animals? God made animals!

What else did God make? God made man! God loved the man and named him "Adam." God gave Adam a special job. What do you think it was?

God told Adam to name the animals. But—oh my! Look at all the animals! Fuzzy, furry, tiny, tall—how could Adam name them all? “Elepottamus”? “Kangamoo”? What should he call them? What would you do?

Adam named the animals, and God was pleased. Then God gave Adam a helper. Adam named her "Eve."

Everyone had a special name. Did you know God has a special name for you? God calls you—His!

God said, "I have called you by your name; you are mine." (Isaiah 43:1)

Prayer Time

Let's thank God for all His love
and watchful care from up above.

Thank You, Lord, for Your great love
and for sending it from up above.
We're glad You gave us each a name
and love all of us just the same!
Amen.

Sleep Time

Tonight's Bible word is *name*. Think about your nice name and all the special names of your family and friends. Good night!

Noah Obeys God

Genesis 6:5–7:16

God looked at the earth. He saw people everywhere disobeying Him. The people didn't love God. They didn't do anything God said. God was very sad. Did anyone love God? Yes! Noah loved God!

God would make it rain and rain. God would wash the world clean. But God loved Noah and would keep him safe.

"Build a boat," said God. So Noah obeyed God. *Zzz—bang-bang-BANG!* Noah built a boat called an ark. God sent special guests to ride in the ark. Who were they? Fuzzy, fluffy, feathery, friendly animals! God sent every kind of animal.

Into the ark went the animals.
Into the ark went Noah and his family.
Then—*whump!*—God closed the door.
God made it rain and rain. God washed
the earth clean. But God kept Noah and
his family and all the animals safe and sound.
Drip, drip, drop—God's love will never stop!

God said, "Make yourself an ark," and Noah obeyed Him. (Genesis 6:14)

Prayer Time

Let's thank God for all His love
and watchful care from up above.

Dear God,

We know You love us. And we love You too. Help us obey You in all that we do.

Amen.

Sleep Time

Tonight's Bible word is *obey*. Think about how happy you feel when you obey God. Night-night!

God's Promise

Genesis 7:11–8:12

Drip, drop, pouring down—rain was falling all around!

God promised to wash the world clean. And God promised to keep Noah, his family, and the animals safe in the ark—and God did. God always keeps His promises! But there was so much water!

Drip, drip, drop—would the rain ever stop?

Yes! God promised to stop the rain—and God always keeps His promises. God stopped the rain. Then God sent a wind to blow across the water. *Ooo-ooo!* The wind blew and blew. It swirled and whirled around, and the flood began to go down, down, down—just as God had promised!

Noah opened the window. The sunshine came in, and a dove flew out. Noah sent the pretty bird to find dry land.

Guess what the bird found! The bird found a green leaf! Noah knew there was dry land. Noah was thankful to God. God had kept His promise!

God remembered Noah, as well as all . . . that were with him in the ark. (Genesis 8:1)

Prayer Time

Let's thank God for all His love and watchful care from up above.

Dear God,

Thank You for Your promises—each one You always keep. Promise now to keep me safe tonight while I'm asleep.

Amen.

Sleep Time

Tonight's Bible word is *promise*. Think about God's promise of love. Sleep tight!

Noah Thanks God

Genesis 8:13–9:17

The flood was finished. The world was clean. Noah was thankful for dry land. Noah was thankful everyone on the ark was safe. And Noah was thankful they could come out of the ark! The door opened up—*CRRREAK*—then what a parade there was!

Lions, tigers, zebras too. Hippity-hop, Mr. Kangaroo! Look at the sun shining up above. Let's thank God with all our love! And that's just what Noah did! Can you say, "Thank You, God"?

Oh! Look in the sky. What do you see? God set a rainbow in the sky. God gave us the rainbow as a promise. He promised never to flood the world again. Isn't it wonderful that God always keeps His promises? Let's thank God for His promises!

Then Noah built an altar to the LORD. . . . God blessed Noah and his sons. (Genesis 8:20; 9:1)

Prayer Time

Let's thank God for all His love
and watchful care from up above.

Dear God,

We want to thank You for all You are and all You do; for Your great care and love so deep, and for Your angels as we sleep.

Amen.

Sleep Time

Tonight's Bible words are *thank You*. Think about all the things you can thank God for. Night-night!

The Oh-No Tower

Genesis 11:1–9

Long ago, people thought they were very smart. They said, "There's no one smarter than us, not one! We're smarter than God—or any-one!" But were they smarter than God? Oh, no! God is smarter than anyone.

The people wanted to be like God. So they built a tall, tall, touch-the-sky tower. Up and up they piled the bricks. And as they worked, they said, "There's no one wiser than us, not one! We're wiser than God—or anyone!" But were they wiser than God? Oh, no! God is wiser than anyone.

The tower was tall. The people were happy. But was God happy? Oh, no! God came down and scrambled the people's words around. The people could not understand each other. They spread out. They went all about! The people learned that no one is wiser than God. Oh, yes!

God said, "For as heaven is higher than earth,
so my ways are higher than your ways,
and my thoughts than your thoughts." (Isaiah 55:9)

Prayer Time

Let's thank God for all His love
and watchful care from up above.

Dear God,
You're the wisest in every way.
We will follow You each day.
Amen.

Sleep Time

Tonight's Bible word is *wise*.
Think about how wise God is
and how He helps us every day.
Sleep tight!

Abraham Trusts God

Genesis 12:1–9; 15:5–6

Abraham and Sarah lived in a comfy-cozy house. One day, God told Abraham to move to a new land. God would lead the way. Abraham didn't want to move. But Abraham trusted God. What do you think Abraham did?

Abraham packed! Abraham packed this; Sarah packed that—they took all their clothes and their little orange cat. Then march, march, march—Abraham and Sarah followed God. And they trusted God too. What a parade it was!

God led Abraham and Sarah to a new land. God was happy that Abraham trusted Him. Abraham looked up. What did he see? Trillions of twinkly stars! Then God promised Abraham that his family would be as many as the stars in the sky. That's a big family!

God said, "I will make you into a great nation, . . .
I will make your name great,
and you will be a blessing." (Genesis 12:2)

Prayer Time

Let's thank God for all His love
and watchful care from up above.
Dear God,
We're glad to know You love us so.
Please help our trust in You to grow.
Amen.

Sleep Time

Tonight's Bible word is *trust*. Think about how nice it feels to trust God and know He loves us. Good night!

A Baby for Sarah

Genesis 18:1–15; 21:1–7

Abraham and Sarah were sad. They wanted a baby. They wanted a baby to cuddle and love. God promised Abraham that his family would be as many as the stars, but still there was no baby. Poor Abraham and Sarah.

One day, three special guests came to visit. The guests said Sarah would have a baby. Sarah smiled. Sarah grinned. Then Sarah laughed.

"I'm too old for babies!" Sarah laughed and said with a wink.

Will God keep His promise? What do you think?

Look—a baby! God kept His promise. God gave Abraham and Sarah a baby boy to cuddle and love. They named the baby “Isaac.” Then Abraham and Sarah thanked God for keeping His promise. What a happy family!

God said, "Is anything impossible for the LORD?"
(Genesis 18:14)

Prayer Time

Let's thank God for all His love
and watchful care from up above.

Dear God,

Thank You for Your promises—we know they all come true. That's because You love us all—and, God, we love You too!

Amen.

Sleep Time

Tonight's Bible word is *promises*. Think about God's promises and how much He loves you. Night-night!

Baby in a Basket

Exodus 2:1–10

Baby Moses needed a safe place to hide. But where? Mother and Miriam, Moses' sister, thought and thought. Mother got an idea! She wove a grassy basket to put her baby in! What did Mother do then?

Mother put baby Moses in his cozy basket. Then she set the basket in the tall, cool grass by the river. Miriam peeked through the grass to make sure baby Moses was safe. Peekaboo! We see you, baby Moses!

Oh! Someone's coming! Who could it be?

A princess! The princess picked up the precious baby. Miriam asked the princess if she wanted help with the baby. Whom did Miriam get to help? Baby Moses' mother!

Everyone was so happy. Mother and Miriam and Moses could be together again.

"Sleep tight, baby Moses," Mother said. "I'll cuddle you and stay right here, and God will keep you safe, my dear!"

God said, "I will save you." (Jeremiah 30:10)

Prayer Time

Let's thank God for all His love
and watchful care from up above.

Dear God,

Our Father up above, You keep us safe with all Your love. We don't ever have to fear because You are always near.

Amen.

Sleep Time

Tonight's Bible word is *safe*. Think about how good it is to know God watches over us. We're safe because God loves us. Sleep tight!

Moses—God's Helper

Exodus 3:1–15

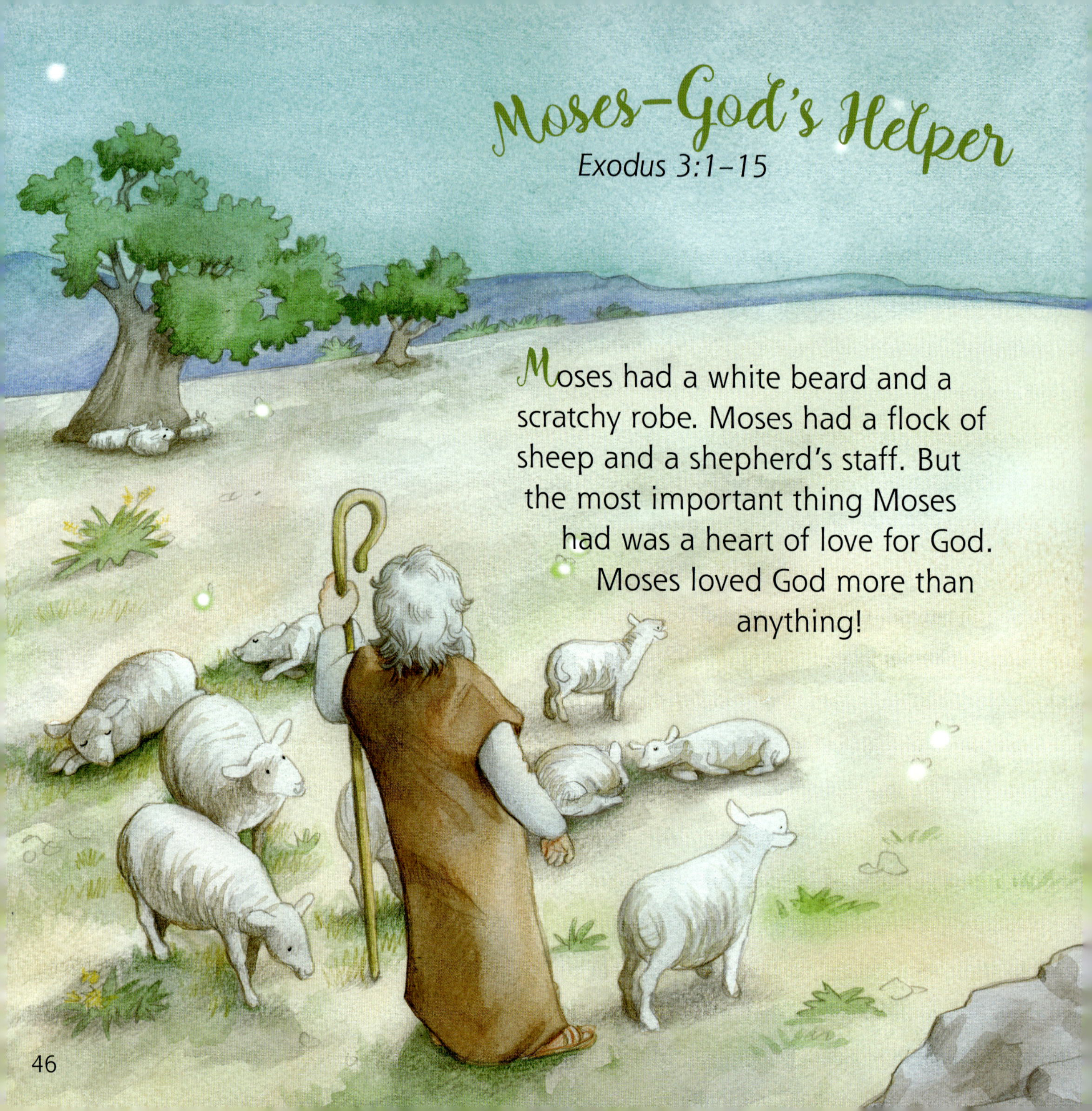

Moses had a white beard and a scratchy robe. Moses had a flock of sheep and a shepherd's staff. But the most important thing Moses had was a heart of love for God. Moses loved God more than anything!

One evening, Moses saw a bright glow on the side of the mountain. "Oh me, oh my—what can it be? I'll climb up the mountain to see what I see!" What do you think Moses saw?

Moses saw a bush with fiery flames—but the bush did not burn up! Then Moses heard someone say his name. Who talked to Moses? God talked to Moses. What do you think He said?

God told Moses he had an important job to do. God told Moses to set His people free from the mean king. God told Moses to be His special helper. Then what did Moses say?

Moses said, "I'll be God's helper—special and true. I'll do all the things God tells me to do.
I know God will help me wherever I go.
Being God's helper says, 'I love God so!'"

God said, "I will certainly be with you." (Exodus 3:12)

Prayer Time

Let's thank God for all His love
and watchful care from up above.

Dear God,
I want to obey You and be Your special helper too.
Amen.

Sleep Time

Tonight's Bible word is *helper*. Think about the ways you can be God's special helper. Good night!

Red Sea Run

Exodus 14:5–31

Once there was a mean king. He didn't like God's people, and he didn't like God. But God loved His people and would keep them safe. So God told Moses to lead His people away from the mean king. The mean king was angry and chased them!

Run, Moses, run—lead God's people free!
Run, Moses, run—but what about the sea?

The Red Sea was very big. The Red Sea was very deep. How could they get across? How could God's people get safely to the other side?

Run, Moses, run—lead God's people free!
Run, Moses, run—but what about the sea?

Could the sea stop God? No, sirree!

God did an amazing thing.

WHOOSH! God split the sea in half! Moses and God's people walked safely to the other side. Then Moses thanked God for keeping them safe.

Walk, Moses, walk—God set you free.
God can do anything—yes, sirree!

That day the LORD saved Israel from the power of the Egyptians. (Exodus 14:30)

Prayer Time

Let's thank God for all His love
and watchful care from up above.

Dear God,

Thank You for Your power and Your awesome might. You keep us safe always, whether day or night.

Amen.

Sleep Time

Tonight's Bible word is *safe*. Think about God's love and how He keeps us safe. Sleep tight!

God Gives Us What We Need

Exodus 16

God loved Moses. God loved His people. But when God helped them escape from the mean king, the people didn't say, "Thank You, God." Instead, they grumbled and groaned and mumbled and moaned.

"We're hungry!" they said. "We want something to eat! Doesn't God love us?"

Yes, God loves us all. And God gives us what we need. So God sent the people something yummy to eat. What did God send? God sent manna! God sent His people delicious bread from heaven. Manna was flaky. Manna was sweet. Yum-yummy manna—God's special treat!

Every morning and every night God sent food for His people to eat. God gave His people manna when they were hungry. God always gives us what we need. Why? Because God loves us! Can you think of all the things God gives you?

God said, "You will know that I am the LORD your God." (Exodus 16:12)

Prayer Time

Let's thank God for all His love
and watchful care from up above.
Dear God,
Thanks so much for all You give
to help us grow and love and live.
Amen.

Sleep Time

Tonight's Bible word is *give*.
Think about all the special things
God gives us. Night-night!

God's Ten Rules

Exodus 20:1–21

Moses loved God. And Moses obeyed God. When God called Moses up the mountain, Moses obeyed. When God told Moses to speak to the people, Moses obeyed. And when God told Moses to listen, Moses obeyed. What did God tell Moses? God gave Moses ten special rules to obey:

God told us He is God and we should worship only Him.
God told us not to make any statues to worship.
God told us to love Him and respect His name.
God told us to take a day of rest.
God told us to love our mommies and daddies.
God told us never, ever to murder anyone.
God told us husbands and wives should be true to each other.
God told us not to steal.
God told us not to lie.
And God told us to be happy with what we have.

Then God wrote His
rules on two stone tablets.
What good rules to obey!

Why did God give us special rules? God gave us rules because He loves us. God gave us rules to keep us safe and happy. And God gave us His special rules to obey. When we obey God's rule, we show that we love God. Thank You, God! Thank You for Your special rules!

God said, "Be careful to do as the LORD your God has commanded you." (Deuteronomy 5:32)

Prayer Time

Let's thank God for all His love
and watchful care from up above.

Dear God,

Your rules help us every day. Help us trust them and obey.

Amen.

Sleep Time

Tonight's Bible word is *rules*. Think about rules that keep us safe and how happy God is when we obey Him. Good night!

God Helps Joshua

Joshua 6:1–20

Joshua was God's brave soldier. Joshua knew God would always help him. There was a city called Jericho. The people there didn't love God. So God decided to give Jericho to Joshua and His people. But my, oh my! There was a big, tall, can't-get-over-it wall around the city! How could Joshua get over that wall? God would help!

God told Joshua, all the soldiers, and all the priests to march around the wall. Right foot, left foot—step, step, step! God told them to march around the wall seven times. Round and round they all marched. 1, 2, 3, 4, 5, 6, 7!

Then God told them to blow their horns. *Tootle, toot*—what a sound! *Tootle, toot*—and the walls fell . . .

DOWN!

Tumble tower, tumble down—till every brick is on the ground!

God brought that tall wall down! Joshua, all the soldiers, and all the priests shouted with joy to God. God had helped them! And God helps us too. Thank You, God!

God said, "Look, I have handed Jericho, its king, and its best soldiers over to you." (Joshua 6:2)

Prayer Time

Let's thank God for all His love
and watchful care from up above.

Dear God,

We're glad You're always there to help us out because You care!

Amen.

Sleep Time

Tonight's Bible word is *help.*
Think about how God helps you and loves you. Night-night!

Ruth and Naomi Are Friends

Ruth 1

Ruth and Naomi were good friends. They shared a house, and they shared the work. Ruth swept the floors while Naomi washed the dishes. And Naomi shared God with Ruth. Naomi told Ruth all about God's love. And soon Ruth loved God as much as Naomi did.

Then one day something sad happened. Ruth and Naomi were left alone. Their husbands had died. What should they do? Where should they go? Naomi wanted Ruth to go back home to live with her own family. But would Ruth go?

Oh, no! Ruth loved Naomi and wanted to stay with her. Ruth knew that God brings us good friends, and friends stick together. So Ruth stayed with Naomi. Ruth and Naomi were friends forever!

Wherever you go, I will go, and wherever you live, I will live; your people will be my people, and your God will be my God. (Ruth 1:16)

Prayer Time

Let's thank God for all His love and watchful care from up above.

Dear God,

We thank You for our loyal friends.
Please help us share and care for them.

Amen.

Sleep Time

Tonight's Bible word is *friends.* Think about the good friends God has given you. Good night, friend!

Samuel Listens to God

1 Samuel 3

Samuel was a little boy who loved God. Samuel lived in the temple with Eli the priest. Samuel like the temple. He had good food. He learned about God. And Samuel even had a comfy little mat to sleep on.

One night, Samuel was sound asleep. He heard someone call his name—"Samuel. Samuel!" Who was calling Samuel? Was it Eli?

"It wasn't me," said Eli. "Close your eyes and go to sleep." So Samuel went to sleep. But soon—"Samuel. Samuel!" Who was calling Samuel? Was it Eli?

"It wasn't me," said Eli. "Close your eyes and go to sleep." So Samuel lay down again. But soon—"Samuel. Samuel!" Who was calling Samuel?

It was God! God talked to Samuel, and Samuel talked to God.

"Speak, God, I am listening," said Samuel.

Samuel listened to God, then Samuel went to sleep.

Sleep well, Samuel! God has special work for you to do!

The LORD came, stood there, and called as before, "Samuel, Samuel!" Samuel responded, "Speak, for your servant is listening." (1 Samuel 3:10)

Prayer Time

Let's thank God for all His love
and watchful care from up above.

Dear God,

Please help me listen to You
wherever I am, whatever I do.

Amen.

Sleep Time

Tonight's Bible word is *listen.* Think about how important it is to listen to God. Good night.

God Chooses David

1 Samuel 16:1–13

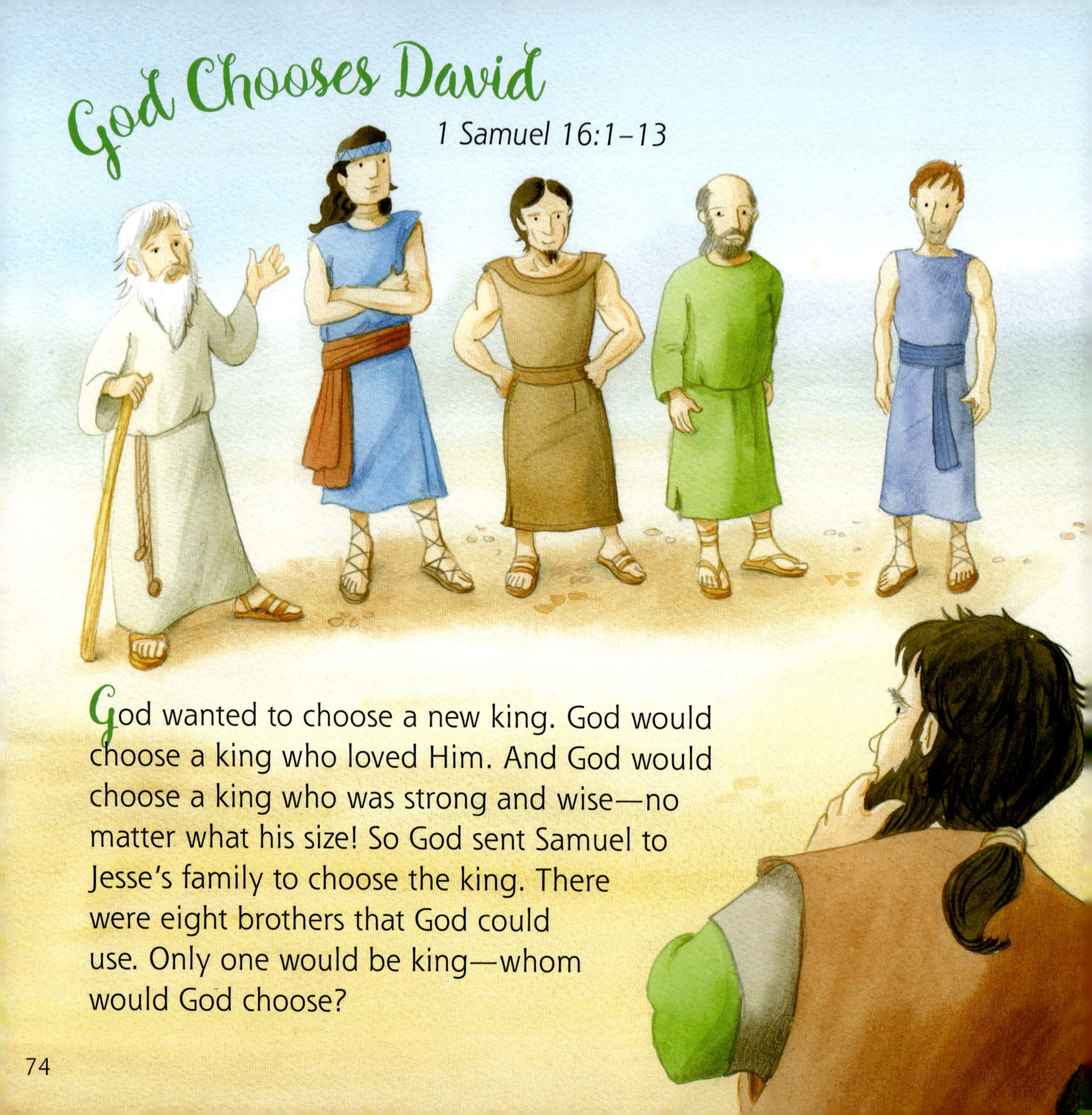

God wanted to choose a new king. God would choose a king who loved Him. And God would choose a king who was strong and wise—no matter what his size! So God sent Samuel to Jesse's family to choose the king. There were eight brothers that God could use. Only one would be king—whom would God choose?

The tall one with the wavy black hair? Or the stronger brother who was standing there? Would God choose the brother who was the oldest? Or would He pick the thinnest or bravest or boldest? Maybe the brother with new leather shoes? Only one could be king—whom would God choose?

God chose David, the littlest brother! God picked David because David was wise and strong and he loved God. God didn't look at how small David was. God looked at David's heart. And David's heart was BIG! His heart was filled with love for God. Hooray for King David!

God said, "The LORD sees the heart." (1 Samuel 16:7)

Prayer Time

Let's thank God for all His love
and watchful care from up above.

Dear God,

We know You are very wise to see our hearts and not our size. Please help our faith in You to grow as we choose to love You so.

Amen.

Sleep Time

Tonight's Bible word is *heart.* Think about how God sees the love in your heart. Night-night.

David and Goliath

1 Samuel 17:1–50

David had seven brothers. David wasn't as big as his brothers. And David wasn't as strong as his brothers. David was the littlest brother of all! But David loved God. And David knew God was bigger and stronger than anyone or anything.

Goliath was a big, BIG guy—and a meanie. Goliath didn't love God. Goliath laughed at God and said, "No one's bigger or stronger than me!"

No, no, Goliath! God is bigger and stronger than anyone! David wanted to stop Goliath from laughing at God. But David was so little—what could he do?

David asked for God's help. Then David took a smooth stone from the ground. He swung his sling round and round, and—*zing! plop!*—Goliath fell down! God helped David topple the mean giant.

Yay, David! Yay, God! Let us clap, and let us sing. God is bigger than anything!

The battle is the LORD's. (1 Samuel 17:47)

Prayer Time

Let's thank God for all His love
and watchful care from up above.

Dear God,

We are glad You're who You are—so big and full of might! You keep us safe the whole day long and in our sleep at night.

Amen.

Sleep Time

Tonight's Bible word is *strong*. Think about how strong God is. Night-night!

David Thanks God

Psalm 23

God always helped David and kept him safe. David loved God and wanted to thank Him. But how could David say, "Thank You, God"? David had an idea. He could pray! This is what David prayed:

"I love You, God. You're stronger than anything and wiser than anyone. The whole world is in Your hands. Thank You, God!"

But David wanted to thank God even more. David had an idea. He could play the harp! David could play his little harp to thank God for His love. This is what David played:

Plink, plinka-plink!
Plinkity-plinkity-plink!

But David wanted to thank God even more! David had an idea. He could write a poem to God. This is what David wrote:

"Dear God, You are my shepherd. You give me all I need. You help me and keep me safe. I'm never afraid because You are with me. You give me such good gifts, God! I'm so happy that I'll be with You always. Thank You, God!"

David worshiped and thanked God for His love.

Thank You, God. We love You!

The LORD is my shepherd. (Psalm 23:1)

Prayer Time

Let's thank God for all His love
and watchful care from up above.

Dear God,

We are glad You're always there
and that You love us and You care.

Amen.

Sleep Time

Tonight's Bible word is *thanks.* Think about the ways you can say, "Thank You, God." Sleep tight.

Smart Solomon

1 Kings 3:5–15

Solomon was David's son. He loved God very much. He became the king of God's people. One night in a dream, God told King Solomon that he could have anything he wanted. God asked, "What should I give you?"

What did Solomon want? What would you want? Shiny jewels? Money galore? Golden coins to count and store? Lots of friends? Leather shoes? A big new house? What would he choose?

Then Solomon remembered that he was king! He was king over lots of people. How could he help all those people? Suddenly, Solomon knew what he wanted!

Solomon wanted to be wise! If King Solomon were wise, he could help lots of people. God was happy with Solomon's choice. He gave Solomon great wisdom. Then God gave King Solomon riches and honor too. King Solomon was wise for loving God!

God said, "I will give you a wise and understanding heart." (1 Kings 3:12)

Prayer Time

Let's thank God for all His love and watchful care from up above.

Dear God,

We know You are very wise. Help us be wise like You. Guide us with Your loving care in everything we do.

Amen.

Sleep Time

Tonight's Bible word is *wise*. Think about how wise it is to love and follow God. Sleep tight.

Daniel Prays

Daniel 6

Daniel loved God very much. He prayed to God day and night. Daniel worked hard and did great things in the kingdom.

King Darius saw Daniel's work and was happy. He wanted to put Daniel in charge of his whole kingdom! But some other men were jealous. They didn't want Daniel to be in charge. So they plotted and planned. What do you think they did?

The men went to King Darius and said, “O King Darius, you are so great and true. People should pray only to you!”

So the jealous men had King Darius write a law that said, “NO PRAYING TO GOD FOR 30 DAYS.” But Daniel loved God and kept praying every day.

When King Darius heard this, he was sad. Because of the law, he would have to punish Daniel. Do you know what the punishment was?

Daniel was tossed in the lions' den with growly-scowly lions! Daniel was afraid, but he kept praying to God. Daniel said, "Dear God, I'll always pray to You no matter what men say or do!"

As Daniel prayed, the lions growled and scowled and snarled! But God answered Daniel's prayers. God sent an angel to close the lions' mouths. Then King Darius knew God is more powerful than anything!

King Darius told all the people to pray to God. And what did Daniel do then? He prayed!

Thank You, God!

He rescues and delivers . . . for he has rescued Daniel from the power of the lions. (Daniel 6:27)

Prayer Time

Let's thank God for all His love
and watchful care from up above.

Dear God,

We bow our heads to pray and say we love You every day.

Amen.

Sleep Time

Tonight's Bible word is *pray.* Think about how good it is to pray to God. Night-night.

Brave Queen Esther

Esther 2:15–5:8; 7

Esther was a very beautiful lady. She was a Jew, one of God's people. Esther loved God very much. The king chose Esther to be his queen. Esther was glad to be queen, but one thing made her sad.

Haman was the king's helper. He didn't love God, and he didn't love God's people. Haman even wanted to hurt God's people! Naughty, naughty Haman!

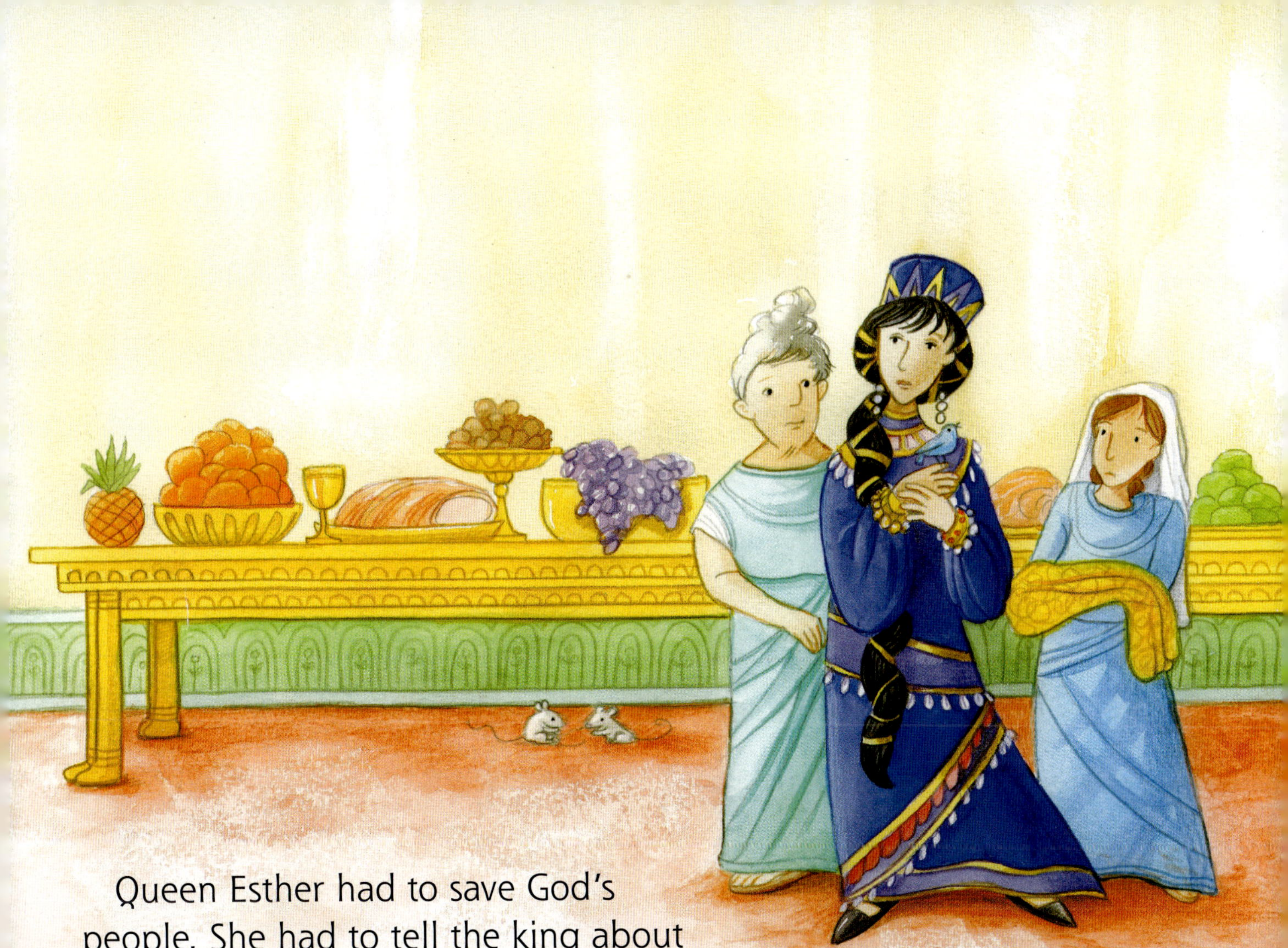

Queen Esther had to save God's people. She had to tell the king about Haman. But Esther was very afraid! What if the king became angry with her? Queen Esther loved God. She wanted to help God's people. But would God help Esther?

He did! God helped Queen Esther be brave and courageous. She told the king, and guess what! The king wasn't angry with Esther at all. He was angry with Haman!

Queen Esther had saved God's people. Hooray for brave Queen Esther! Hooray for God!

In God I trust; I will not be afraid. (Psalm 56:4)

Prayer Time

Let's thank God for all His love
and watchful care from up above.
Dear God,
You are with us all day long.
Please help us be brave and strong.
Amen.

Sleep Time

Tonight's Bible word is *brave.* Think about how strong and brave we can be with God's help. Good night.

God Answers Jonah

Jonah 1–3

The people of Nineveh didn't obey God. God told Jonah to tell the people, "Obey Me." But what did Jonah say? "Oh, no! I won't go!" Jonah did not want to talk to the mean people. So Jonah ran and hid from God. No, no, Jonah! You can't hide from God!

Jonah was thrown into the sea. *Kersplash!* He sank down, down, down, until—*glip-glup*—a big fish swallowed him up! For three days and nights, Jonah sat in the belly of the fish. It smelled pretty awfulish!

Jonah was sorry he'd disobeyed, so Jonah just sat there and prayed and prayed. Jonah told God he was sorry. Jonah thanked God for saving his life. And Jonah told God he loved Him. But did God answer Jonah's prayers?

Yes, He did! God always answers our prayers. God made the big fish spit Jonah out on the sand—*pftuwee!* Jonah was safe! Jonah was thankful that God answers our prayers.

What did Jonah do then? He jumped up and ran to Nineveh. Jonah obeyed God!

I called to the LORD in my distress,
and he answered me. (Jonah 2:2)

Prayer Time

Let's thank God for all His love
and watchful care from up above.

Dear God,

Each time we pray to You, we know You'll hear and answer too.

Amen.

Sleep Time

Tonight's Bible word is *answers.* Think about how God hears and answers all your prayers. Night-night.

The New Testament

Happy Birthday, Jesus!

Luke 2:4–7

What a quiet night it was! Mary and Joseph walked along the road. Mary smiled. She knew God's promise was near. Mary knew that the baby she would have was God's greatest promise. But Mary was tired. So was Joseph. *Yawwwn!*

After a while, they came to the town of Bethlehem. Where could they rest? Where could the special baby be born? Joseph asked his family for a place to stay, but there were no more rooms inside.

But God was watching—He would care. And He did. God led them to a cozy stable.

Then late one night, just before morn . . .

God's tiny baby Son was born! Mary wrapped Him in a blanket tight, and Jesus slept in a manger that night. In that still, quiet night, God sent His Son to us.

God promised the world a Savior and Prince of Peace. And God always keeps His promises! Jesus came to save us. Jesus came to give us peace. And Jesus came to love us.

Happy Birthday, Jesus! We love You too.

God said, "They will name him Immanuel," which is translated "God is with us." (Matthew 1:23)

Prayer Time

Let's thank God for all His love
and watchful care from up above.

Dear God,

Thank You for sending Your Son from above. Jesus is our Prince of Peace and the One we love.

Amen.

Sleep Time

Tonight's Bible word is *Jesus.* Think about the special night when Jesus was born and how much God loves us. Sleep tight.

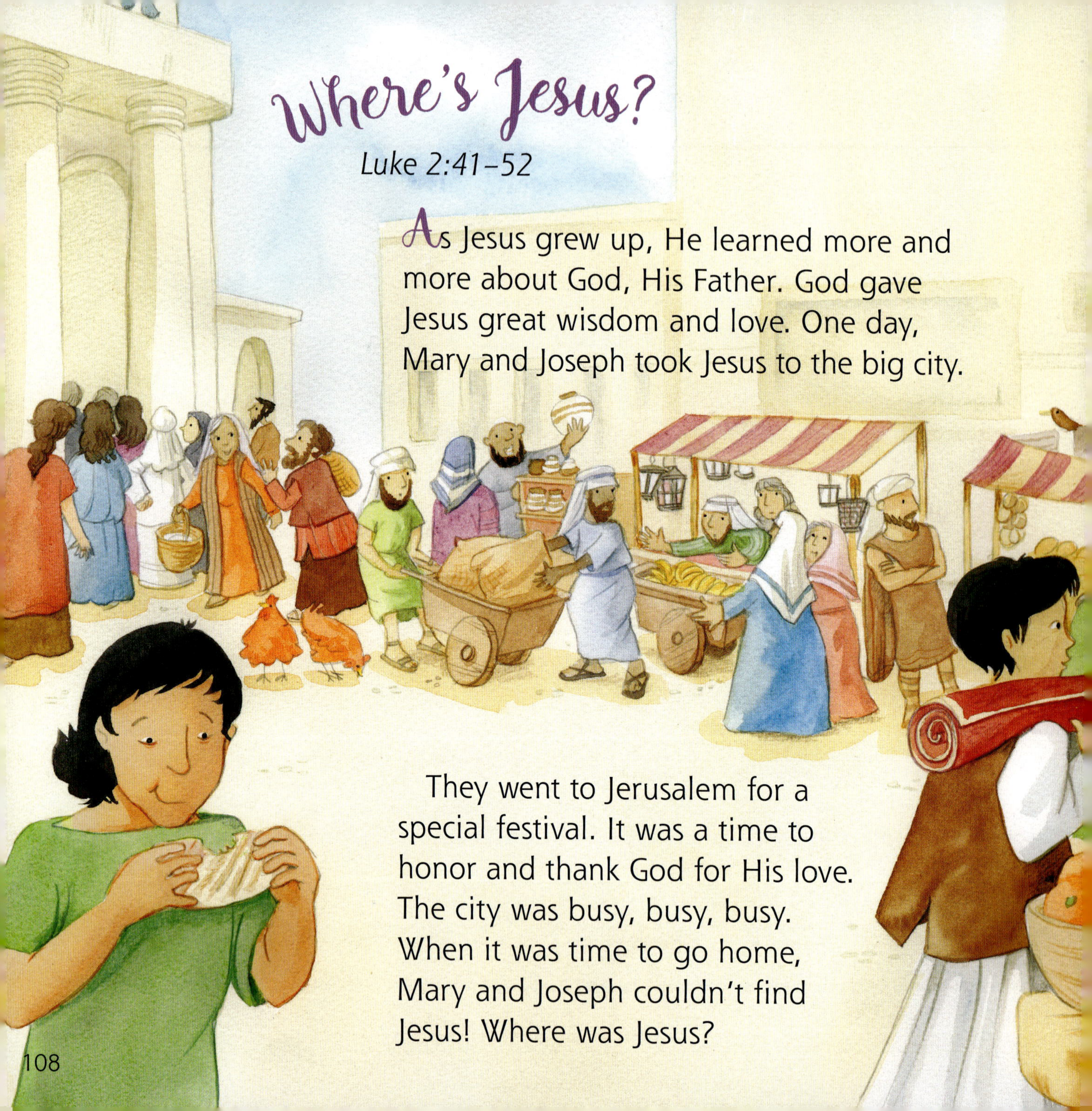

Where's Jesus?

Luke 2:41–52

As Jesus grew up, He learned more and more about God, His Father. God gave Jesus great wisdom and love. One day, Mary and Joseph took Jesus to the big city.

They went to Jerusalem for a special festival. It was a time to honor and thank God for His love. The city was busy, busy, busy. When it was time to go home, Mary and Joseph couldn't find Jesus! Where was Jesus?

Mary and Joseph were so worried—back and forth they searched and scurried! They looked for Jesus in the square. They searched for Jesus everywhere. But they couldn't find Him anywhere! Where was Jesus?

Jesus was in the temple! Jesus was talking with the teachers. What were they talking about? They were talking about God! Jesus was asking questions and giving answers. People were learning about God. Jesus was happy to be learning about God. And Joseph and Mary were happy to find Jesus!

Jesus increased in wisdom and stature, and in favor with God and with people. (Luke 2:52)

Prayer Time

Let's thank God for all His love
and watchful care from up above.

Dear God,

*Please help us learn about You—
about the Bible and Jesus too.*

Amen.

Sleep Time

Tonight's Bible word is *learn*.
Think about how happy God
is when we learn about Him.
Night-night.

Jesus Is Baptized

Matthew 3:13–17

One day, Jesus went to the Jordan River. What did Jesus see? Jesus saw a man baptizing people in the water. That man was John the Baptist. His clothes were made of camel's hair. He was talking to the people there. John told the people they had done wrong things. John told the people they should be sorry. And John told the people they could tell God they were sorry by being baptized in the water.

Jesus wanted to be baptized. He walked into the water. John the Baptist said, "Oh, no, Jesus! You should be baptizing me instead!" But Jesus knew that God wants everyone to be baptized. And Jesus always obeyed God.

So John baptized Jesus in the Jordan River.

Then what did Jesus see?

Jesus saw the Spirit of God! God's Spirit came down from heaven like a dove and rested on Jesus. God said He was very happy with Jesus, His Son. Then John the Baptist and everyone knew that it was right to be baptized.

We make God happy when we obey Him, just like Jesus did!

God said, "This is my beloved Son, with whom I am well-pleased." (Matthew 3:17)

Prayer Time

Let's thank God for all His love
and watchful care from up above.

Dear God,

Jesus always obeyed You. Please help us obey You too.

Amen.

Sleep Time

Tonight's Bible word is *obey*. Think about how Jesus obeyed God and how we can obey Him too. Good night.

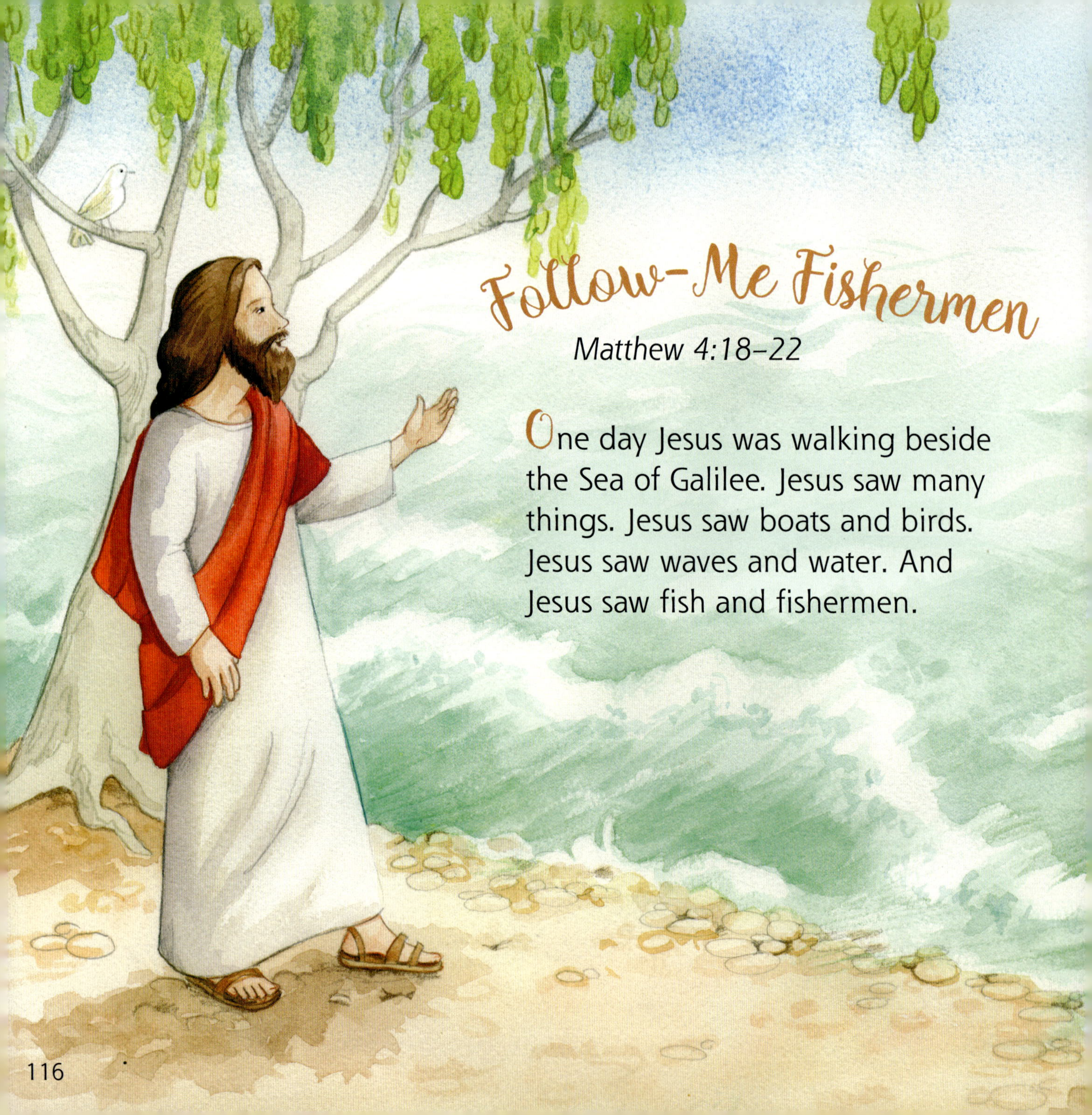

Follow-Me Fishermen

Matthew 4:18–22

One day Jesus was walking beside the Sea of Galilee. Jesus saw many things. Jesus saw boats and birds. Jesus saw waves and water. And Jesus saw fish and fishermen.

Two of the fishermen were brothers. Peter and Andrew were catching fish in their nets. They looked up and saw Jesus walking toward them.

Jesus looked at them and said, "Come, follow Me, and I will make you fish for people."

At once, Peter and Andrew dropped their fishing nets. They wanted to go with Jesus. They wanted to follow Him and learn about God.

Where did they go?

They went to look. They went to find more people who wanted to know, love, and follow Jesus.

We can be like Peter and Andrew. We can follow Jesus too! And we can tell other people about Him!

Jesus said, "Follow me." (Matthew 4:19)

Prayer Time

Let's thank God for all His love
and watchful care from up above.

Dear God,

Please help us to follow You in all we say and all we do.

Amen.

Sleep Time

Tonight's Bible word is *follow.* Think about how we can follow Jesus and learn about Him. Good night.

Love Everyone

Matthew 5:43–48

Jesus came to love us. Jesus came to teach us. And Jesus came to teach us about love!

One day Jesus was teaching many people on a hillside. Look at all the people! Every-one knew that Jesus was wise. And everyone knew that Jesus taught God's truth. What did Jesus teach them?

Jesus said to love everyone! Jesus said to love all people no matter what they say or do. Even the ones who never share? Yes! Even the ones who pull our hair? Yes! Even the ones who scowl and frown? Yes! And even the ones who push us down? Yes! Yes! YES! Jesus said to love other people as we love ourselves.

Jesus wants us to love all people no matter what they say or do. When we love others, it shows Jesus that we love Him too. So when you meet someone, here's what you can do—shake hands, smile, and say, "Jesus and I love you!"

Jesus said, "Love one another." (John 13:34)

Prayer Time

Let's thank God for all His love
and watchful care from up above.

Dear God,

You are so amazing! Your love is like no other. Please help us be good and kind and show love to each other.

Amen.

Sleep Time

Tonight's Bible word is *love.* Think about all the people you can love and how you can love them the way Jesus wants you to. Sleep tight.

Jesus Stops the Storm

Luke 8:22–25

One day, Jesus and His friends climbed into a boat. Birds chirped. The wind blew softly. Waves rocked the little boat back and forth, back and forth. *Yawwwn*—Jesus was sleepy. He lay down and fell fast asleep. *Shhh!* Don't wake Jesus.

Then all of a sudden—*boom, crash, BOOM!* What a storm! The rain drummed—*ratta-tat-tat!* The wind blew—*ooo-ooo-ooo!* Water splashed into the boat. Jesus' friends were afraid. They woke Jesus.

"What if we sink? What if we drown? How can You sleep with the rain pouring down?"

What did Jesus do?

Jesus said, "Wind, stop! Waves, stop!"

Did the wind and waves obey Him? They did! The waves stopped flowing. The wind stopped blowing. Everyone was safe.

Jesus' friends asked, "Who is this who can stop a storm?"

Who is this? It's Jesus! Jesus keeps us safe so we don't have to be afraid. Thank You, Jesus!

Jesus said, "Don't be afraid." (Matthew 10:31)

Prayer Time

Let's thank God for all His love
and watchful care from up above.

Dear God,

We're glad for Jesus' love that's free to all You've made. We know with Jesus by our sides, we'll never be afraid.

Amen.

Sleep Time

Tonight's Bible word is *safe*. Think about how God keeps you safe all day and all night. Night-night!

Dinner for 5,000

John 6:1–14

Look at all the people! The people were listening to Jesus. They were learning about God and His love. But—*grumble, grumble*—their tummies were hungry!

Where could they eat? Where would they find food? Jesus' friends were worried. So many people, so many hungry tummies! What would Jesus do?

Andrew saw a little boy with a food basket. What's in the basket? Tasty bread and yummy fish. The little boy wanted to share his meal with Jesus. What a nice little boy! But how could five loaves of bread and two small fish fill so many hungry, grumbly tummies? What would Jesus do?

Jesus thanked God for the food. Then He divided it for all the people. Jesus made the meal big enough to feed everyone. Then what a picnic they had! Yum-yummy, food filled every tummy! Jesus fed all those hungry people with one little boy's meal. The boy shared his food and his love too!

Would you share your lunch with others? Would you share your love with others? What would Jesus do?

Jesus said, "Freely you received, freely give."
(Matthew 10:8)

Prayer Time

Let's thank God for all His love and watchful care from up above.

Dear God,

Please help us always share and give to show we really care.

Amen.

Sleep Time

Tonight's Bible word is *give*. Think about what you can give to others to show them God's love. Sleep tight.

The Good Samaritan

Luke 10:25–37

Jesus told a story about a man who was robbed. Mean men stole the man's money and left him lying hurt in the road. Ouch! The poor hurt man! Who would help him?

Step, step, step. A village priest came along, but he didn't stop—he just went on! There's a hurt man lying there, but who will stop to offer care?

Step, step, step. A Levite man came along, but he didn't stop—he just went on! There's a hurt man lying there, but who will stop to offer care?

The priest didn't help the man. The Levite didn't help the man. Would anyone help him?

Clip-clop, clippity-clop. A Samaritan came riding on a donkey. *Clip-clop, clippity-clop*. The Samaritan was the one to stop! The good Samaritan gave the man water to drink and covered his wounds. Then the good Samaritan took the hurt man to town and paid for his care. What a nice man!

Jesus wants us to show we care and to help when someone needs us there.

Jesus said, "Be merciful." (Luke 6:36)

Prayer Time

Let's thank God for all His love
and watchful care from up above.

Dear God,
We are glad You're always there.
Help us show how much we care.
Amen.

Sleep Time

Tonight's Bible word is *mercy*. Think about how happy Jesus is when we're kind and show mercy to others. Good night.

The Wise Builder

Matthew 7:24–27

Jesus told a story of two builders—one was wise, and one was not. See if you can tell which builder was so smart. The first builder built his house on sand—slippery-groundy, slidey-downy sand. Uh-oh! The other builder built his house on hard rock—rough and rigid, really rugged rock. Ahhh! When the builders were done, each thought he was the best builder who ever built! But then the rains came.

Whoosh, whoosh—the rains came down, and the house on the sand tumbled down to the ground! But the house built on stone didn't budge, bend, or moan! That house stood stock-still on that rock on the hill!

Who was the smartest builder? The one who built his house on the rock! When troubles came, the house stood firm and didn't fall.

Did you know that we're builders too? We can be wise builders when we build our lives on Jesus. When we trust and love Jesus, we can be strong like the house on the rock!

Jesus said, "Everyone who hears these words of mine and acts on them will be like a wise man who built his house on the rock." (Matthew 7:24)

Prayer Time

Let's thank God for all His love
and watchful care from up above.

Dear God,

Please send help from up above
to build our lives on Jesus' love.

Amen.

Sleep Time

Tonight's Bible word is *build.* Think about how good it is to build our trust in Jesus. Sleep tight.

The Lost Sheep

Luke 15:3–7

Jesus once told a story about a shepherd who had 100 sheep.

One day, the shepherd counted his sheep: "96, 97, 98, 99—my, oh my! There's one I can't find!" One of the sheep was lost! The shepherd had many more sheep, but he loved every one of them. "I'll find my sheep—I'll look high and low. But where should I start? I just don't know!"

The shepherd looked behind a stone. He searched beside the brook. The sad, old shepherd searched the fields. Oh, where else should he look? The shepherd looked up in a tree and behind a dandelion. He searched and sought his little sheep—he'd never stop his tryin'!

"Oh, can you help me find my lamb? I really love him so! Do you see my little lamb? If so, please let me know!"

There he is! The shepherd was so happy to find his little sheep that he whooped with joy—oh, boy! He brought his sheep back to the flock then had a party to celebrate.

God is like that shepherd. He wants us to stay close to Him all the time. Why? Because He loves us—every one!

Jesus said, "Rejoice with me, because I have found my lost sheep!" (Luke 15:6)

Prayer Time

Let's thank God for all His love
and watchful care from up above.

Dear God,

We want to be near Your love and You—to keep us safe our whole lives through.

Amen.

Sleep Time

Tonight's Bible word is *near.* Think about how God wants to be near you and how good it feels to be close to God. Good night.

He Can Walk!

Matthew 9:1–8; Mark 2:1–12; Luke 5:18–26

Once there was a man who couldn't walk. The man would lie on his mat all day and night. The man's friends said, "Jesus can help you!" The friends believed in Jesus and His power. So they took the man to see Jesus. Do you think Jesus helped him? Let's see!

Jesus looked at the man who couldn't walk. Jesus looked at the man's friends. And Jesus saw their faith! Jesus knew the friends believed in His power and love. That made Jesus very happy! Then Jesus said to the crippled man, "You're forgiven. Get up, take your mat, and go home!"

What do you think happened then?

The man stood up and walked! The man who had never walked could skip and jump and walk and run. Everyone praised Jesus. The people were very surprised, but not the man's friends. They trusted Jesus. They had faith in Jesus' power. And they believed that Jesus could do anything.

We can trust and believe in Jesus too!

Jesus said, "Believe in God; believe also in me." (John 14:1)

Prayer Time

Let's thank God for all His love
and watchful care from up above.

Dear God,

Please help us to trust in You and
have more faith our whole lives through.

Amen.

Sleep Time

Tonight's Bible word is *believe.* Think about how much we trust and believe in Jesus' love. Night-night!

Jesus Loves Children

Matthew 19:13–15; Mark 10:13–16

Jesus was teaching the grown-ups. Jesus was teaching them about love. All the mommies and daddies wanted their little girls and boys to be close to Jesus.

But Jesus' friends said, "Oh, no—make them go! Jesus is too busy!"

What did Jesus say?

Jesus said, "Come to Me." Jesus wanted the little children near. Jesus hugged the children and loved them. Jesus wanted the little children to learn about God. So all the children came to Jesus. Big kids, small kids, freckled-nosed tall kids, sad kids, happy kids, giggling-wiggling glad kids, kids with black hair, kids with brown, kids from every tent and town; they all came to Jesus!

Why did Jesus want the little children to come to Him? Because Jesus loves little children. Jesus loves each boy and girl—every child around the world! And Jesus knows children love Him too.

Thank You, Jesus. We do love You!

Jesus said, "Let the little children come to me." (Mark 10:14)

Prayer Time

Let's thank God for all His love
and watchful care from up above.

Dear God,

Thank You for Jesus' love. We love Him so much too. Please help us find ways to say, "Jesus, we love You!"

Amen.

Sleep Time

Tonight's Bible word is *love.* Think about how Jesus loves all little children and how He loves you too! Sleep tight.

Zacchaeus Is Forgiven

Luke 19:1–10

Once there was a grump named Zacchaeus. "Hummmph! No one likes me!" said Zacchaeus. The people didn't like Zacchaeus because he took their money for taxes. Zacchaeus heard that Jesus was coming to town. Everyone was happy. But Zacchaeus didn't understand. "Hummph! Why does everyone love Jesus? Guess I'll take a peek!" he said.

What did Zacchaeus do? Zacchaeus climbed a tall tree! He peeked through the branches.

When Jesus came to the tree, He said, “Zacchaeus, come down. I’m going to your house.”

Zacchaeus slid down the tree—*zooop!* Everyone stared. Everyone was surprised! Why would Jesus want to eat with grumpy Zacchaeus?

Jesus ate with Zacchaeus because Jesus loved Zacchaeus! And Jesus forgave Zacchaeus for the mean things he'd done.

Do you know what happened then? Zacchaeus was so happy. He gave back the people's money. Yay, Zacchaeus!

Jesus said, "For the Son of Man has come to seek and to save the lost." (Luke 19:10)

Prayer Time

Let's thank God for all His love
and watchful care from up above.

Dear God,

Thank You for forgiving us when we disobey. Help us forgive others in the same special way.

Amen.

Sleep Time

Tonight's Bible word is *forgive.* Think about people you can forgive and how happy it makes God. Night-night!

Give to God

Luke 21:1–4

Jesus was at the temple with many people. The people were thanking God for His love. The people gave offerings and gifts to God. What did the rich people give to God? Gold and silver and precious jewels. *Clink, clink, clinkety-clink!* They gave much to God—but still had much left.

Then Jesus saw a poor widow. She was dressed in tattered robes and her shoes had holes. What could this poor woman give to God? She had no gold or silver or precious jewels. All she had were two copper coins—*clink, clink!* The woman had just two pennies to give, but she gave everything to God.

Who gave more to God—the rich people or the poor woman? The poor woman gave more because she gave all she had. She gave out of her heart, while the other people gave out of their riches. Jesus was proud of the woman—and Jesus is proud when we give to God too!

Jesus said, "This poor widow has put in more than all of them." (Luke 21:3)

Prayer Time

Let's thank God for all His love and watchful care from up above.

Dear God,

Please help us give to You with everything we say and do.

Amen.

Sleep Time

Tonight's Bible word is *give.* Think about all you can give to God. Good night.

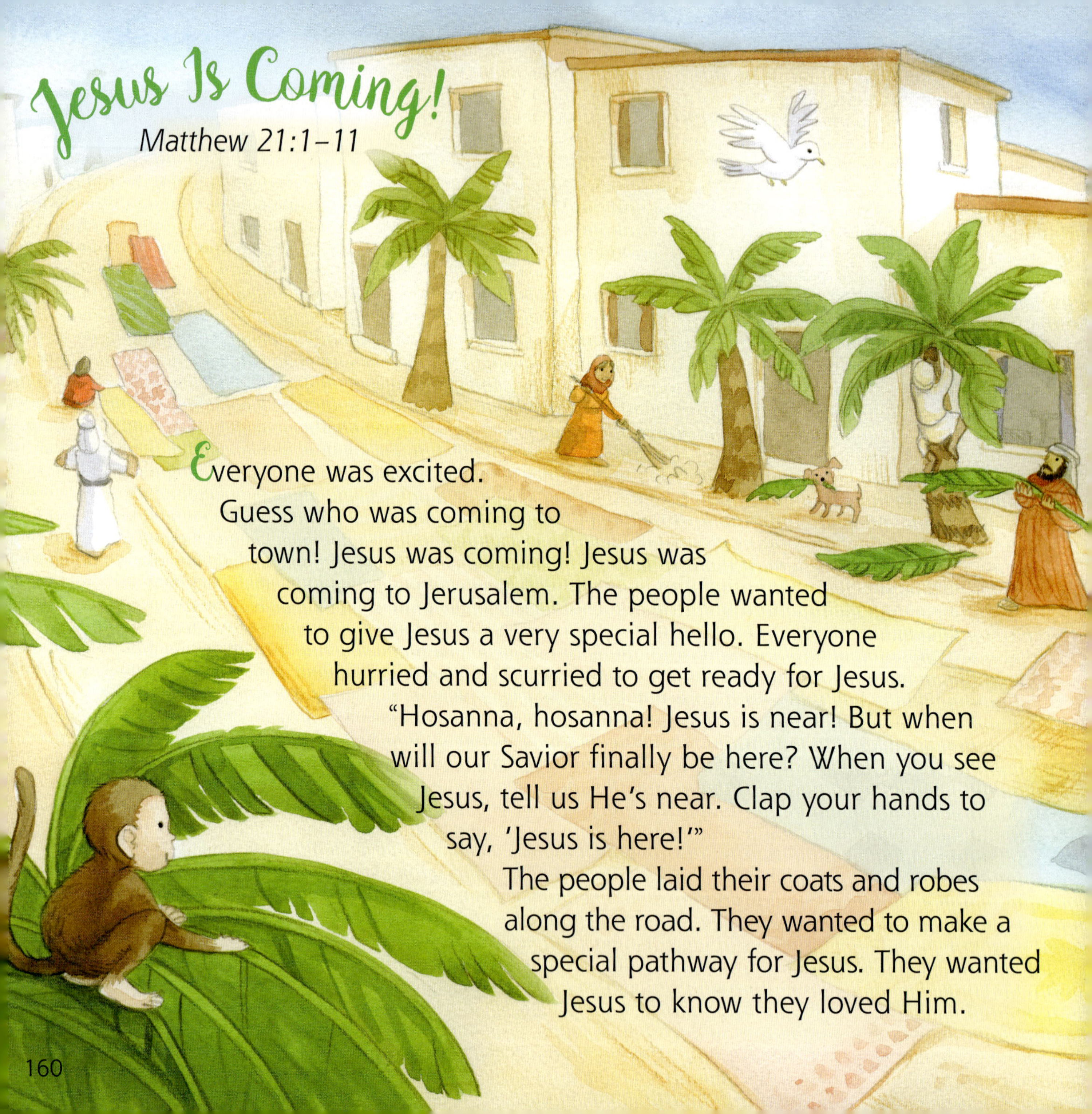

Jesus Is Coming!

Matthew 21:1–11

Everyone was excited. Guess who was coming to town! Jesus was coming! Jesus was coming to Jerusalem. The people wanted to give Jesus a very special hello. Everyone hurried and scurried to get ready for Jesus.

"Hosanna, hosanna! Jesus is near! But when will our Savior finally be here? When you see Jesus, tell us He's near. Clap your hands to say, 'Jesus is here!'"

The people laid their coats and robes along the road. They wanted to make a special pathway for Jesus. They wanted Jesus to know they loved Him.

Then the people picked palm branches to wave. They wanted Jesus to know He was special to them. Oh, how they scurried to get ready for Jesus. Hurry, hurry! Jesus could come any moment!

Here's Jesus! Did you clap your hands? All the people waved palm branches. All the people praised Jesus. All the people showed Jesus their love.

We can show Jesus our love too.

"Hosanna, hosanna! Jesus is here! He lives in our hearts, and we feel Him near!"

Clap your hands and tell Jesus true—
"Jesus, Jesus, we love You!"

Jesus said, "You also be ready, because the Son of Man is coming at an hour you do not expect." (Luke 12:40)

Prayer Time

Let's thank God for all His love
and watchful care from up above.

Dear God,

Thank You that Jesus is near and that our hearts can feel Him here! Help us be ready to tell Him true—"Jesus, Jesus, we love You!"

Amen.

Sleep Time

Tonight's Bible word is *ready*. Think about how you can always be ready to love and follow Jesus. Night-night.

Serve Each Other

John 13:1–17; Mark 14:22–26

It was suppertime. Jesus and His friends sat around the table. It was a very special supper because it would be Jesus' last supper with His friends. Before they ate, Jesus did something surprising. He took a towel and some water and then—Jesus washed their feet! He washed the dusty, dirty feet of all His friends.

When He was finished, He said, "I have served you. Now you should serve each other."

Jesus' friends were so surprised! They sat down at the table. Then Jesus held up a cup to drink from and a loaf of bread. Jesus blessed the cup and bread and served His friends again.

Why did Jesus serve His friends in this special way? Jesus wanted to show how much He loved them. Jesus wanted His friends to serve others. And Jesus wants us to serve others too. When we serve others and do kind things, we show people we love them—and we show Jesus we love Him too!

Friends and family, sister, brother—Jesus said to serve each other!

Jesus said, "I have given you an example, that you also should do just as I have done for you." (John 13:15)

Prayer Time

Let's thank God for all His love and watchful care from up above.

Dear God,

Please help us find a way to serve each other every day.

Amen.

Sleep Time

Tonight's Bible word is *serve*. Think about all the people you can serve and how you can be kind. Sleep tight.

Jesus Died for Us

Matthew 27:11–66; Mark 15:20b–41; Luke 23:26–49; John 19:16–30

Not everyone loved Jesus. Not everyone believed that Jesus was God's Son. Jesus came to help us and teach us. But most of all, Jesus came to love us. Some of the people wanted to hurt Him. But Jesus still loved the people.

They hung Jesus on a cross where He died. Jesus' friends were very sad. They knew He was God's Son. They knew Jesus loved them. But they didn't know why Jesus had to die.

"This is the saddest day—oh my!
Why did Jesus have to die?"
Do you know why?

Jesus died for us! He wants us to live in heaven with Him forever. But we can't get there on our own. We need Jesus to take us home! So Jesus died to forgive our sins, to show us God's love never ends.

We can be God's children too. Jesus died because He loves you!

Jesus said, "Father, forgive them." (Luke 23:34)

Prayer Time

Let's thank God for all His love
and watchful care from up above.

Dear God,

We are so glad that Jesus came to love and forgive us each the same.

Amen.

Sleep Time

Tonight's Bible word is *forgive*. Think about Jesus' love and how good it is to be forgiven. Sleep tight.

Jesus Is Alive!

Matthew 28:1–10; Mark 16:1–10; Luke 24:1–12

Jesus' friends were sad. It had been three days since Jesus died on the cross. Some women who had followed Jesus came to visit the tomb. The women walked along sadly. My, how they missed Jesus!

The suddenly, something amazing happened! At the tomb, the big stone had been rolled away. And what do you think they saw? An angel!

The angel said, "Don't be afraid. I know you're looking for Jesus—but He's not here. Jesus is alive!"

The women peeked inside the tomb. What did they see?

Nothing! The tomb was empty.

"Jesus is alive!" they shouted. They were so happy that they ran to tell Jesus' other friends the good news.

Jesus is alive today!
We're so happy.
Shout, "Hooray!"
Jesus is alive today—
and forever!

Jesus said, "I am with you always." (Matthew 28:20)

Prayer Time

Let's thank God for all His love
and watchful care from up above.

Dear God,
We are so thankful we can say,
"Jesus is alive today!"
Amen.

Sleep Time

Tonight's Bible word is *alive*. Think about how happy you are that Jesus is alive. Night-night.

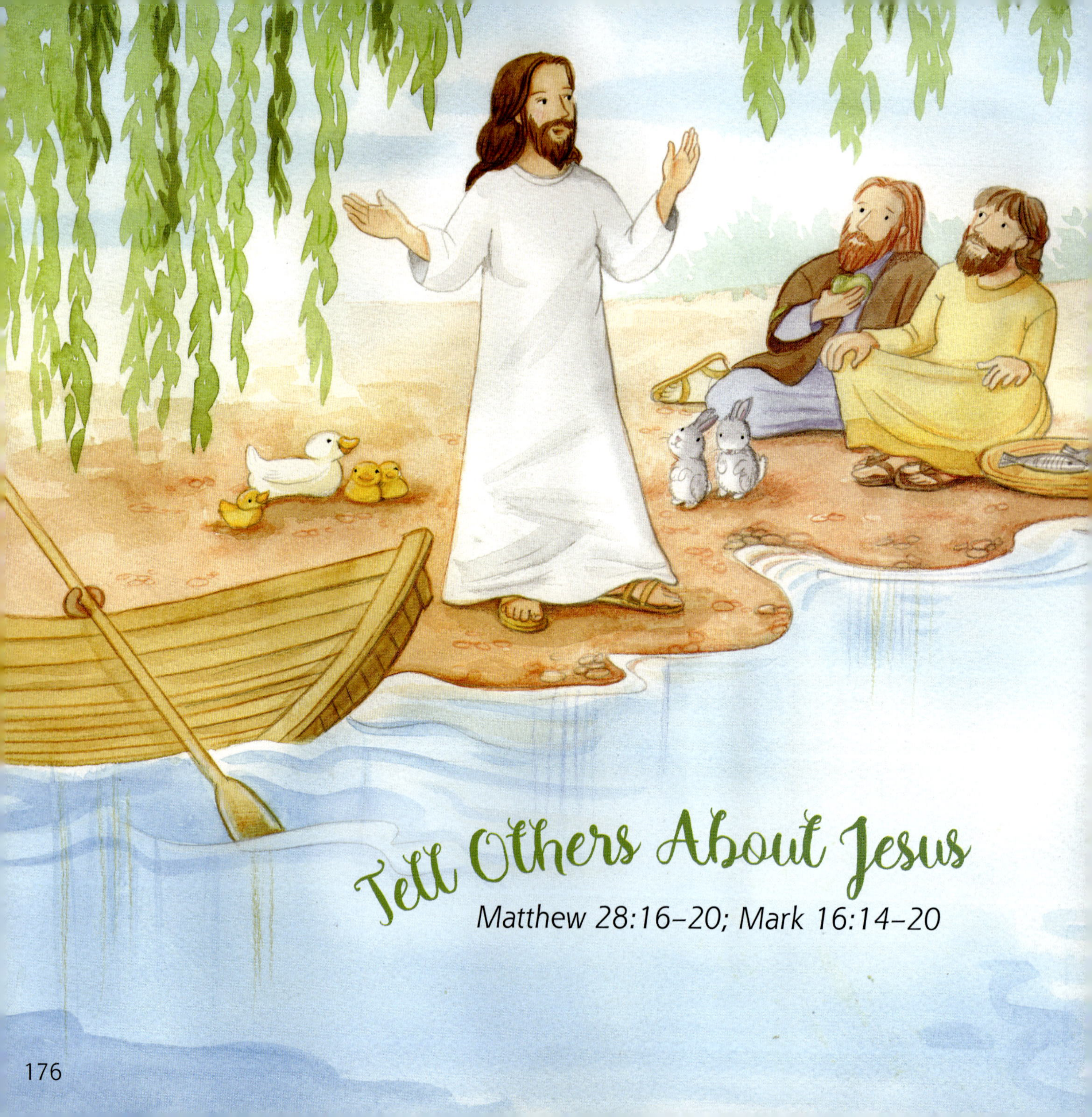

Tell Others About Jesus

Matthew 28:16–20; Mark 16:14–20

Jesus' friends were so happy. They knew that Jesus was God's Son. They knew that Jesus was alive. And they loved Jesus more than ever! Jesus called to His friends and gathered them. What do you think Jesus said?

Jesus told His friends to go all over the world. Jesus told His friends to tell others about His love and forgiveness. And Jesus told His friends to baptize people and help people believe in God. Then something amazing happened!

Jesus was lifted up into the clouds! Where was Jesus going? Jesus was going to live in heaven with God! Jesus' friends were so excited and happy. They started doing what Jesus said right away. Jesus' friends told everyone the good news about Jesus' love and amazing forgiveness!

How many people can you tell about Jesus?

Jesus said, "Go into all the world and preach the gospel to all creation." (Mark 16:15)

Prayer Time

Let's thank God for all His love and watchful care from up above.

Dear God,

Thank You for forgiving us and giving us Your Son. Help us tell of Jesus' gift of love to everyone!

Amen.

Sleep Time

Tonight's Bible word is *tell.* Think of all the people you can tell about Jesus and His love. Sleep tight.

Hello, Holy Spirit!

Acts 2:1–12

Jesus promised to send us a special gift. Jesus promised to send us a special friend and helper. This helper is called the Holy Spirit. Jesus' friends were waiting for the Holy Spirit. They waited, and they prayed. When would the Holy Spirit come? How would they know the Holy Spirit was here? Oh, listen—someone is coming!

Whoooosh! Suddenly there came the sound of a big, BIG wind from heaven! *WHOOOSH!* The sound filled the house where Jesus' friends were sitting. Then flashes like heavenly flames came down, and people started praising God.

"Is this our heavenly friend? Is this the Holy Spirit Jesus said He would send?"

Yes! It was the Holy Spirit! The Holy Spirit came to help us do what Jesus wants us to do. The Holy Spirit came to teach us more about God's love. And the Holy Spirit came so we could serve Jesus with love and courage!

Hello, Holy Spirit! We're so glad to meet You!

Jesus said, "Receive the Holy Spirit." (John 20:22)

Prayer Time

Let's thank God for all His love
and watchful care from up above.

Dear God,

We will be thankful to the end for the Holy Spirit, our special friend.

Amen.

Sleep Time

Tonight's Bible words are *Holy Spirit*. Think about our special friend, the Holy Spirit, and how He helps us. Good night.

Prayer Helps Peter

Acts 12:5–17

Peter was one of Jesus' friends. He loved Jesus and wanted to tell others about Him. But a mean king didn't like Jesus, and he didn't like Peter. So the mean king tossed Peter in jail and chained him to two rough, gruff guards. Poor Peter. How could he ever get free?

Many people loved Jesus, and they loved Peter too. When they heard that Peter was in jail, what did they do? They prayed! They prayed and asked God to set Peter free. Peter prayed too—then fell fast asleep between the two sleepy, snoring guards.

Shhh, be very quiet—God is at work! How would God help Peter escape?

God sent an angel to Peter. The angel told Peter to wake up. Then the chains fell off Peter's wrists. Tiptoe, off we go. Did the mean guards awake? Oh, no, no, no!

God heard the prayers of the people and helped Peter escape. Then Peter was free to tell more people about Jesus. Yay, Peter! Yay, God!

Jesus said, "Ask and you will receive." (John 16:24)

Prayer Time

Let's thank God for all His love
and watchful care from up above.

Dear God,

*We are glad You're always there
to listen to our every prayer.*

Amen.

Sleep Time

Tonight's Bible word is *prayer.* Think about how God hears and answers our prayers. Night-night.

Our New Home

Revelation 21:1–22:5

The Bible tells us what it will be like to live with God and Jesus. Everything will be new! God will make a new heaven and a new earth. God will send a new city down from heaven. But what will the city be like? Let's see!

Look, behold! A city of gold, with gates of gleaming stone. And there is Jesus, full of light, sitting on His throne! The River of Life flows from the throne, along the streets of gold. And there's truth and peace and much more love than anyone can hold!

God will wipe away each tear. There'll be no crying in that place! No sorrow, no pain, no fear—only love and joy and the light of God's face. We'll greet each other with smiles and laughter. With Jesus and God, we'll live happily ever after!

Jesus said, "I am making everything new."
(Revelation 21:5)

Prayer Time

Let's thank God for all His love and watchful care from up above.

Dear God,

Thank You for making everything new—and letting us live with Jesus and You.

Amen.

Sleep Time

Tonight's Bible word is *heaven.* Think about how very beautiful heaven will be. Night-night.

PARENT Connection

Remember

Whatever you do, do it from the heart, as something done for the Lord and not for people.—Colossians 3:23

Read

Reading Bible stories and learning the lessons that God teaches us through them can be lots of fun, but Jesus points out in Mark 10:17–21 that we need to do more than simply know what God says. The rich young ruler knew what all the commandments were, but he still needed to use those lessons in his own life. Knowing what God wants for us is good, but using those lessons in the way we live every day shows that we have faith and trust in God. It also allows us to show God's love to others.

Think

1. Which is your favorite Bible story? What did you learn from it?
2. What are three other lessons that you learned?
3. How can you apply these lessons to your life?

Do

The day after a Bible story is read, talk with your family about ways to use the lesson that day. Then do it! Remember, Bible stories and lessons aren't just for reading—they're for living.